IS A BLUE WHALE THE BIGGEST THING THERE IS?

Robert E. Wells

Albert Whitman & Company
Chicago, Illinois

For my mother, Hester B. Wells

Also by Robert E. Wells
What's Smaller Than a Pygmy Shrew? • How Do You Lift a Lion?
What's Faster Than a Speeding Cheetah? • Can You Count to a Googol?
How Do You Know What Time It Is? • What's Older Than a Giant Tortoise?
Did a Dinosaur Drink This Water? • Polar Bear Why Is Your World Melting?

Library of Congress Cataloging-in-Publication Data
Wells, Robert E.
Is a blue whale the biggest thing there is? / Robert E. Wells.
p. cm,
Summary: Illustrates the concept of big, bigger, and biggest by comparing the physical measurements of such large things as
a blue whale, a mountain, a star, and the universe.
1. Size judgement—Juvenile literature. [1. Size.] I. Title.
BF299.S5W455 1993 93-2703 530.8'1—dc20 CIP AC
ISBN-13: 978-0-8075-3655-1 (hardcover)
ISBN-13: 978-0-8075-3656-8 (paperback)

Text and illustrations copyright © 1993 by Robert E. Wells.
Published in 1993 by Albert Whitman & Company.
Printed in China.
26 25 24 23 22 BP 17 16 15 14 13

Hand-lettering by Robert E. Wells.
The illustration media are pen and acrylic.
Design by Susan B. Cohn.

For more information about Albert Whitman & Company,
please visit our web site at www.albertwhitman.com.

This is a book about the UNIVERSE, and other Very Big Things. So it uses Very Big Numbers—even MILLIONS and BILLIONS.

To remind you just how big those numbers are, try first counting to a smaller number—ONE HUNDRED. At normal speed, that should take about one minute. Keep on counting, and you'll reach a THOUSAND in about 12 minutes.

If you decide to continue counting to a MILLION, don't plan on doing anything else for awhile. Counting for a steady 10 hours a day, it will take about 3 weeks.

If you are REALLY ambitious and would like to count on to a BILLION, you'd better make that your career. Counting 12 hours a day, it will take you more than 50 years!

We hope you enjoy this book. It has some HUNDREDS and THOUSANDS, and LOTS of MILLIONS and BILLIONS. Will it give you big ideas? You can count on it!

This is the tail of a blue whale.
The "flipper" parts are called flukes.

Just the flukes, all by
themselves, are bigger than
most of Earth's creatures.

Here's the WHOLE blue whale. It's not just bigger than MOST of Earth's creatures, it's bigger than ALL of them.

A blue whale can grow to be 100 feet (30 meters) long and weigh 150 tons (136,000 kilograms)! It's the biggest animal that ever lived.

But of course, a blue whale is NOT The Biggest Thing There Is.

If you put 100 blue whales in a really big jar,

and then put two of those whale jars
on an enormously large platform,

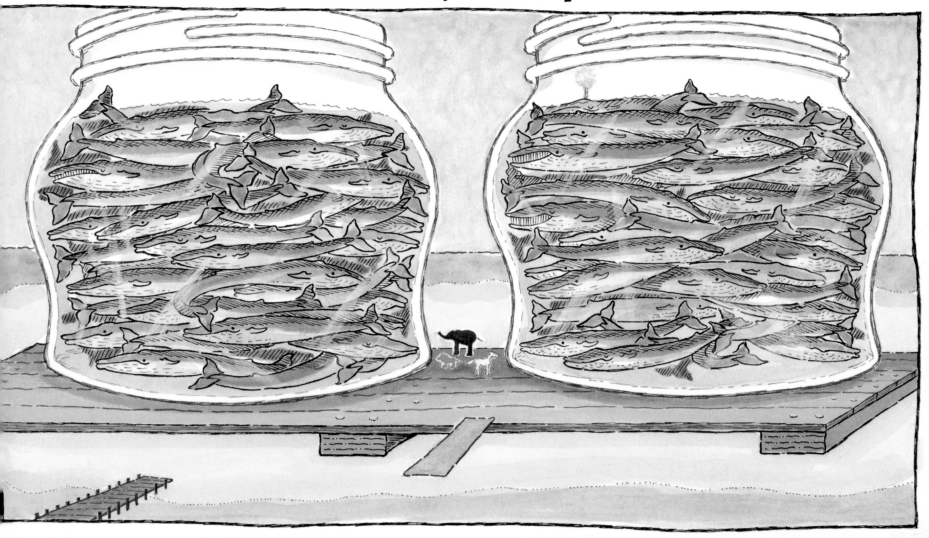

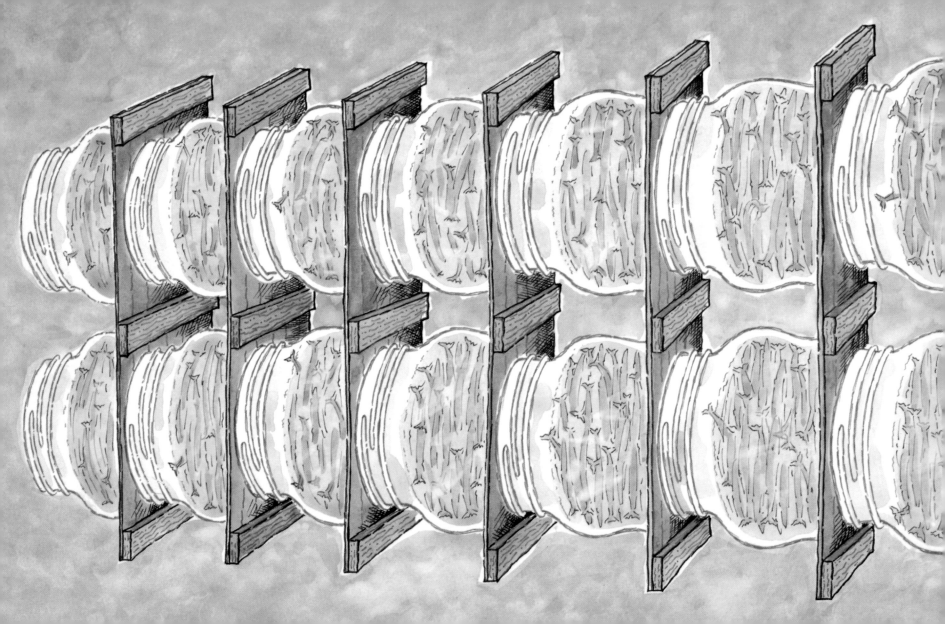

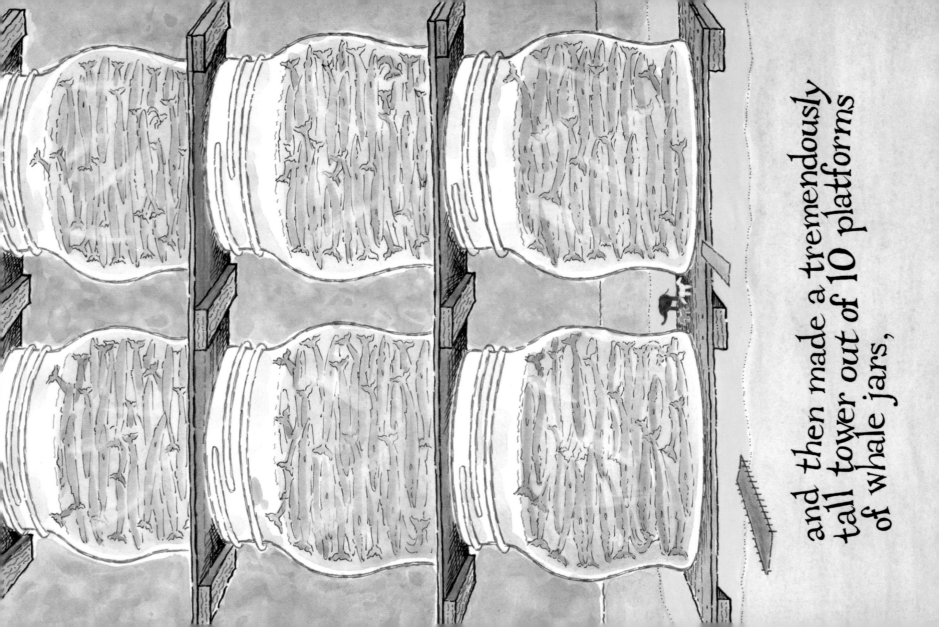

and then made a tremendously tall tower out of 10 platforms of whale jars,

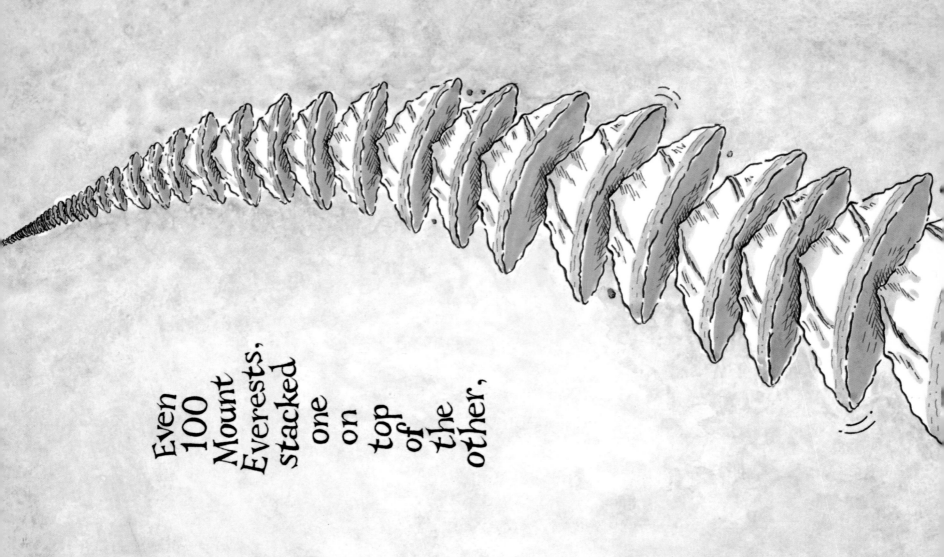

Even 100 Mount Everests, stacked one on top of the other,

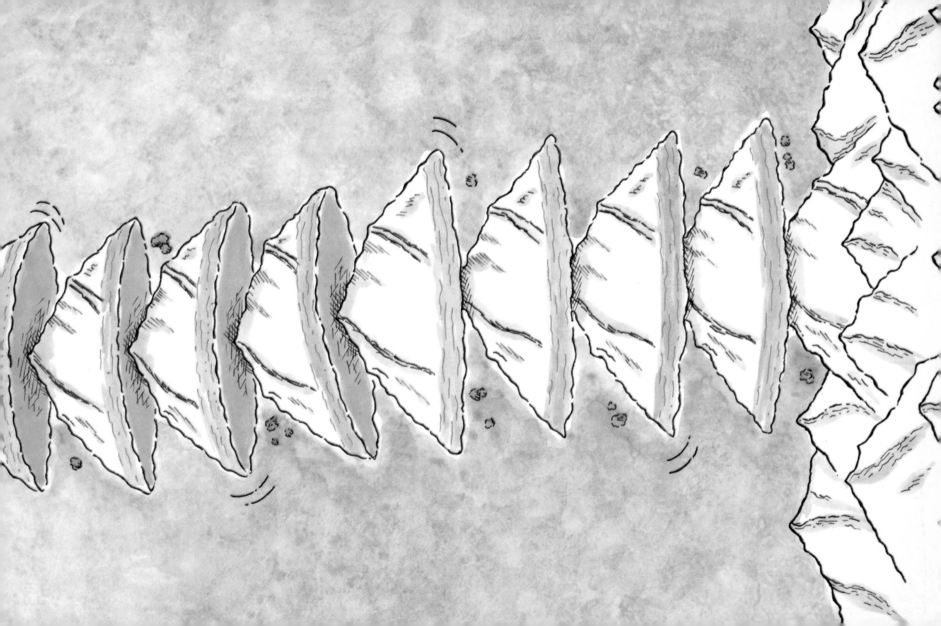

would be a mere WHISKER on the face of the Earth!

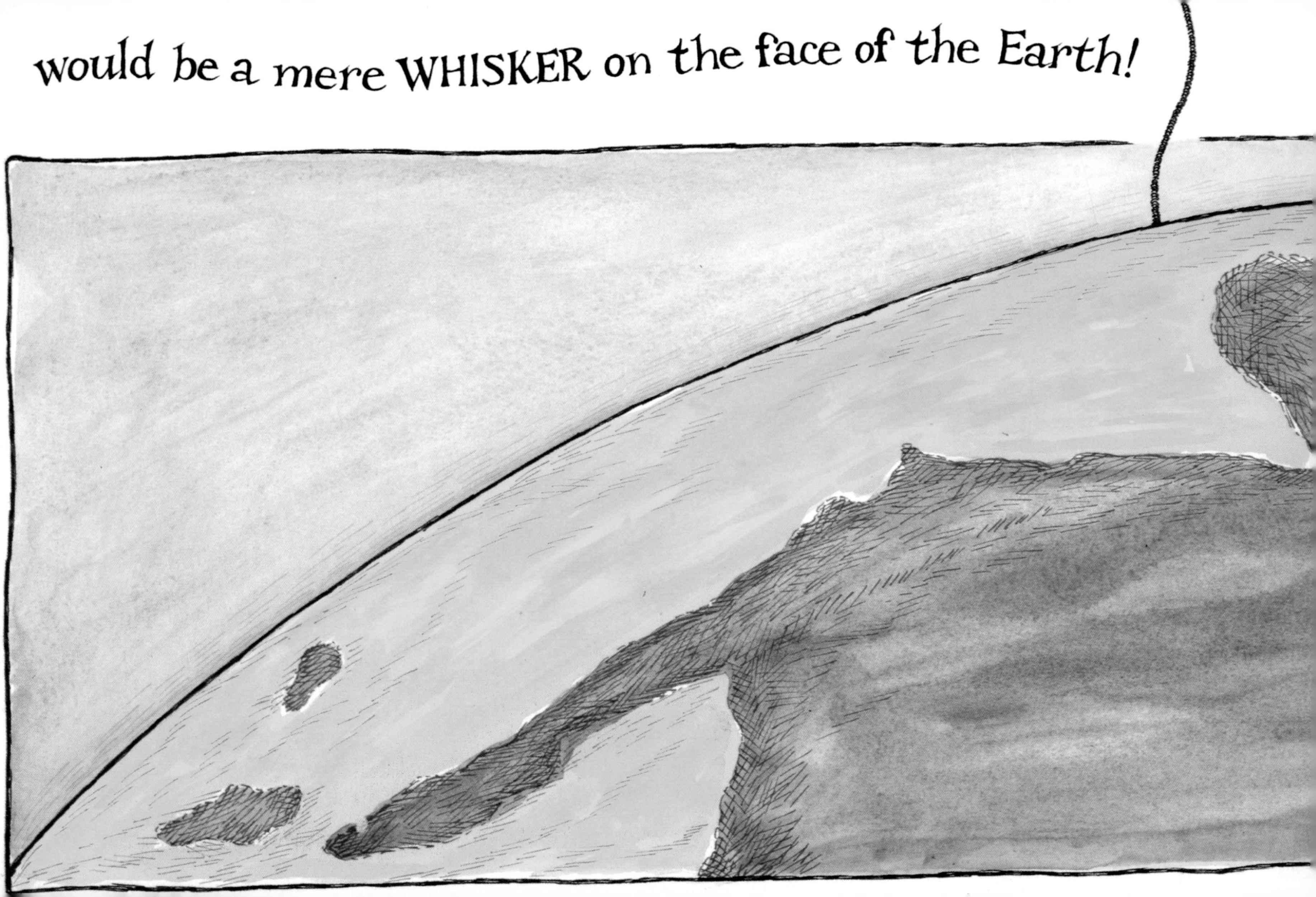

And just in case you thought our EARTH
was The Biggest Thing There Is,

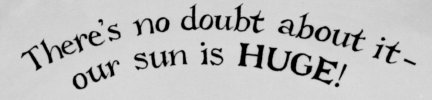

next
to
our
sun!

There's no doubt about it -
our sun is HUGE!

More than
ONE MILLION
of our Earths
would fit inside!

It's so big that it can control the orbits
of nine planets and give us a sunburn
from 93 million miles (150 million
kilometers) away!

But even our SUN is FAR from being
The Biggest Thing There Is

because
if our sun
were turned
into a
SUN-SIZED
ORANGE

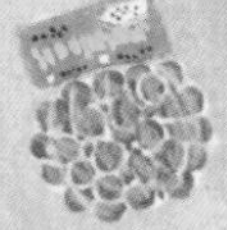

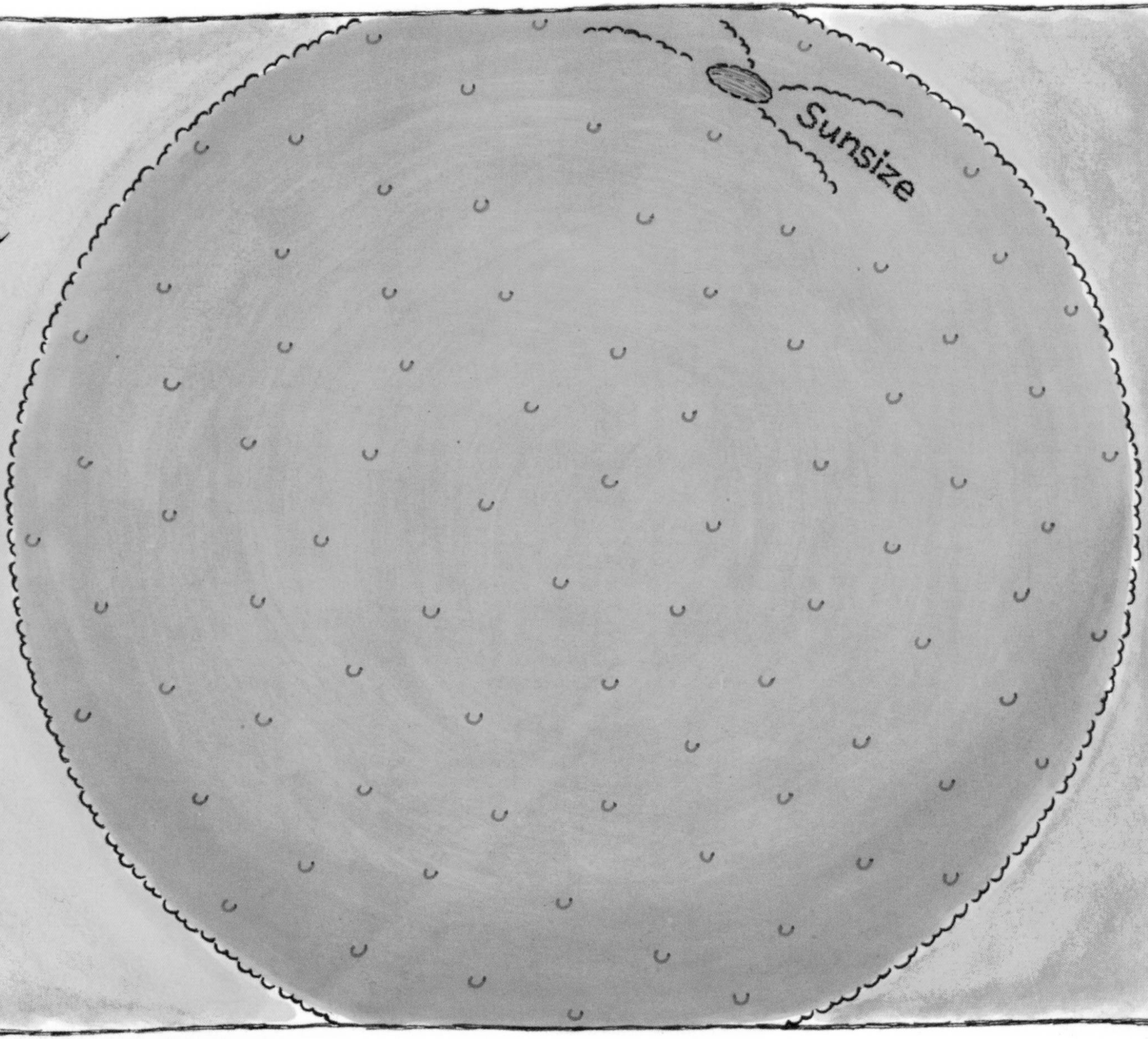

it could be set on top of something
much bigger—a red supergiant
star called ANTARES!

Stars come in many different sizes.
Our sun and Antares are both stars,
but our sun is medium-sized, and
Antares is...well, it's a SUPERGIANT!

Antares was not always this big. All stars
have lifetimes; and some, like Antares, expand
to enormous sizes and turn red as they get
close to the end of their lives.

Antares has grown so big that
MORE THAN FIFTY MILLION OF
OUR SUNS WOULD FIT INSIDE!

How could anything be that big?
How could anything be BIGGER?

Our galaxy, the MILKY WAY, is much, MUCH bigger. A galaxy is a gathering of a great number of stars. The MILKY WAY is made up of BILLIONS of stars, including Antares. Along with those stars, there are countless comets and asteroids, lots of meteors, and at least nine planets!

Just as a sand castle has a shape, formed by all the grains of sand it is made of, our galaxy has a shape, formed by all of its stars.

We cannot see the shape from Earth.
But if we were OUTSIDE our galaxy,
looking at it from a great distance,

it might look something like this, with a bulging galactic center and great cloudlike swirls glowing with the light of billions of stars! From this distance you could not see the galaxy's stars separately.

The Milky Way MUST be The Biggest Thing There Is!

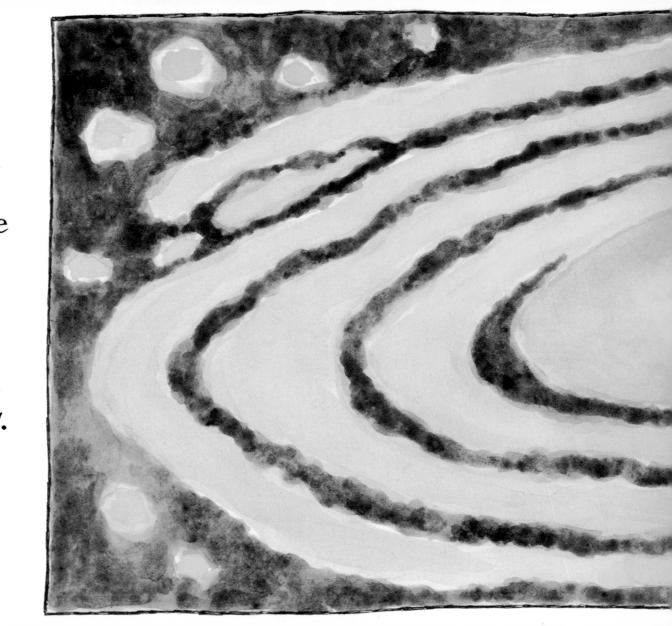

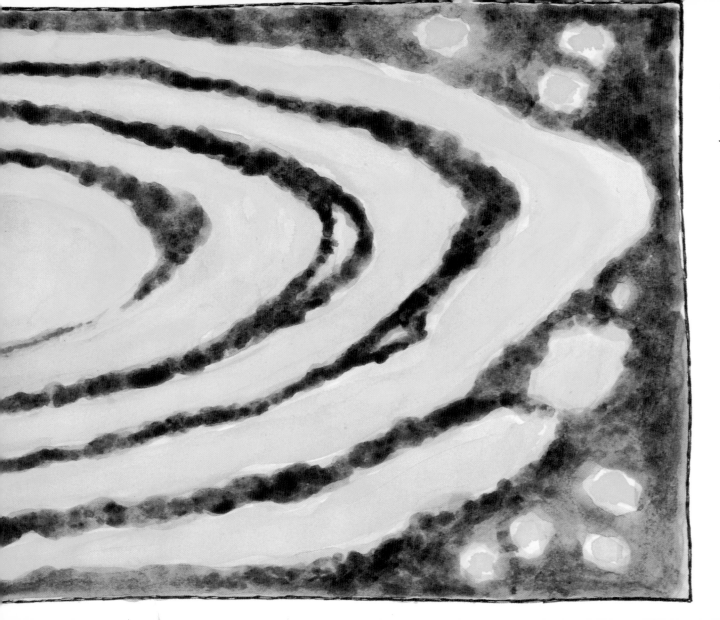

But wait. Our galaxy is not alone. Astronomers, the scientists who study stars, report that there are BILLIONS of OTHER galaxies out in the darkness we call space.

And ALL of them are part of Something Even Bigger—

THE UNIVERSE!

The UNIVERSE is
ALL THE GALAXIES
and ALL THE DARK SPACE
between them.

It is EVERYTHING THAT EXISTS
anywhere in space and time!

Because it is so
AMAZINGLY BIG,
no one knows what
the WHOLE universe
really looks like.

But here's what a tiny part of it
might look like, showing some of
the many different kinds of galaxies.

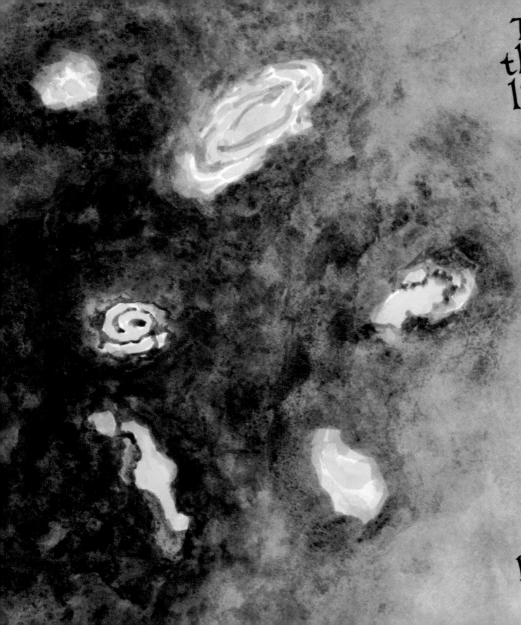

The universe is the biggest thing we know. More than likely, we can call it

THE BIGGEST THING THERE IS.

Even with our most powerful telescopes, we cannot see to the end of the universe. So we don't know how big it really is.

But this much we do know:

it's a lot bigger
than a blue whale.

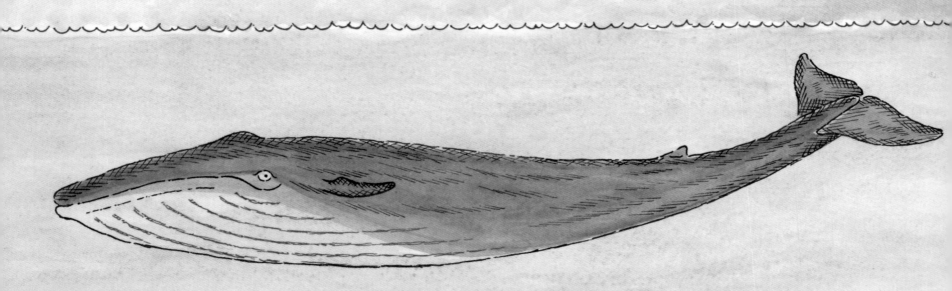

Some additional thoughts on Very Big Things

It's fairly easy to imagine the size of a jar of blue whales, or a stack of Mount Everests, or even a crateful of sun-sized oranges. But imagining the immense size of the universe—that's another matter.

The truth is, the universe is so unbelievably big that even with it's countless billions of stars and galaxies, it is almost totally empty. Vast distances separate stars, even within those gatherings of stars we call galaxies.

If our galaxy were pictured to scale, and our sun were the size of this dot •, the nearest star to it would be another "dot" some ten miles (sixteen kilometers) away, with other "star dots" hundreds, and even thousands, of miles / kilometers distant.

The distances between galaxies are also vast. Like the stars, the galaxies in this book are shown much closer together and more alike in size than they would actually be. Shrinking vast distances proved to be more practical than making a picture book millions of miles / kilometers wide!